Employ Your Tax Dollars

Employ Your Tax Dollars

✦

How Your Business Can Save Money
Using the Workforce Development System

Donna F. Coles **CWDP**
Words@Work Consulting, LLC

iUniverse, Inc.
New York Lincoln Shanghai

Employ Your Tax Dollars
How Your Business Can Save Money
Using the Workforce Development System

Copyright © 2007, 2008 by Donna F. Coles

iUniverse books may be ordered through booksellers or by contacting:

iUniverse
2021 Pine Lake Road, Suite 100
Lincoln, NE 68512
www.iuniverse.com
1-800-Authors (1-800-288-4677)

Because of the dynamic nature of the Internet, any Web addresses or links contained in this book may have changed since publication and may no longer be valid.

The views expressed in this work are solely those of the author and do not necessarily reflect the views of the publisher, and the publisher hereby disclaims any responsibility for them.

ISBN: 978-0-595-44133-4 (pbk)
ISBN: 978-0-595-88457-5 (ebk)

Printed in the United States of America

To all of the small-business owners who want to pursue the American dream and who realize the importance of helping others fulfill their dreams as well. And to some indispensable women: My mother Thelma Hunter, my sister Cathy, my aunt Iris, and my good friends Claudia and Suzanne.

Contents

Introduction:
You've Made the Investment,
Why Not Cash In?

Workforce development (also referred to as employment and training, or "E&T") programs have been a part of the national landscape for several generations. Workforce development professionals are committed to helping our citizens prepare for, obtain, and maintain employment that affords a satisfactory standard of living. Not only do government programs *want* to do business with employers, but in most instances, their funding mandates it. The dilemma? Many small and medium-sized[1] business owners are utterly unaware of the availability of government programs to offset and subsidize hiring and training expenses, and many administrators of government programs don't know how to effectively forge relationships with members of the business community. What results is a large gulf that appears impassable from both sides. Businesses go begging for workers and E&T programs are challenged to meet their clients' needs for jobs.

What the Big Companies Know

Over the years, the Bureau of Labor Statistics has conducted surveys revealing that larger companies regularly utilize government programs to offset the expense of hiring, assessing, and training employees. In a report prepared for the U.S. Small Business Administration in 2001, researchers found that larger firms were more likely, by a margin of four to one, to have heard of and used government training programs.[2] Data support another fact: larger companies, particularly those with one hundred or more employees, are more apt to provide some kind of formalized training to their employees. This ensures that the business will have workers with the skill sets required to do the job effectively. The smallest companies, with less than twenty-five workers, provided 118 hours of training in the first three months of employment, a figure unchanged from 1992 to 2001. The larger companies, however, provided 172 hours of training in 2001, 11 more than the 163 hours reported in 1992.

A more recent study conducted by the Government Accounting Office (GAO) in February 2005 revealed how businesses viewed and utilized One-Stops. One-Stops are comprehensive centers, authorized by the Workforce Investment Act (WIA) of 1998. WIA replaced the previous workforce legislation and put emphasis on increased customer choice as well as universal access to services. The One-Stops provide a continuum of services to help job seekers and businesses meet their employment needs. Generally, the One-Stops are a collaboration of partner organizations that enable a client to access several services in one location. The GAO research indicated that the percentage of businesses aware of and using WIA-funded One-Stop centers had increased over the years. Forty-eight percent of small businesses were aware of the One-Stops, and 21 percent of all small businesses used them, but those figures lagged far behind the 79 percent of businesses with over five hundred employees that knew about and utilized the One-Stop system. The full report, GAO-05-259, which includes the scope and methodology of the study, can be found on the GAO Web site.[3]

The purpose of this publication is to introduce government-sponsored workforce development programs to small and medium-sized businesses. Nearly 90 percent of American businesses have fewer than twenty workers. These "Mom and Pop" establishments will generate the majority of jobs in America in the twenty-first century. The increase of minority-and women-owned businesses is fueling small-business expansion. New immigrants to the United States who open businesses add to these figures, as do retiring baby boomers like me, who are choosing to leave the job market at relatively young ages and are opening businesses in record numbers. As their businesses grow, the new entrepreneurs can take advantage of government programs to offset their hiring and training costs with tax credits, on-the-job training, apprenticeships, customized training, and other programs.

According to a 2003 GAO report, there were forty-four training programs administered by nine federal agencies that provided a range of employment and training services.[4] These programs serve veterans, older workers, youth, people dislocated from their jobs, recipients of public assistance, Native Americans, migrant workers, high school graduates, dropouts, and senior citizens. Just about everyone at one time or another can benefit from such programs. Programs that provide workforce development services include those administered by the Departments of Labor, Housing and Urban Development, Health and Human Services, Agriculture, Education, and others. The programs are so widespread, they can assist virtually all Americans to meet *some* of their needs when seeking work or skills training assistance. Despite the ubiquitous existence of workforce development programs, they are usually mischaracterized by the middle class or business class. These programs are often associated with the poor, or with persons who possess what is often referred to in E&T jargon as "barriers to employment," which are defined as the conditions that contribute to an individual having difficulty establishing strong attachments to the workforce. Examples of those considered to have "barriers to employment" are single parents, high school dropouts, people with disabilities, people whose first language is not English, and people who receive public assistance. In one illustration, a workforce professional who was making a presentation to a group of human resource representatives asked how many of them had utilized the public E&T system to fill job vacancies. Of two hundred, only five had done so. The workforce professional remarked, "it became clear that those attending this conference (employer staffing experts and company recruiters) considered the Workforce Development system as a place where lower-skilled people go to get help in finding a job—and of no particular value for recruiters that are trying to find highly skilled 'A' and 'B' players for their company."[5]

Misconceptions aside, I have provided training to entrepreneurs, professionals with annual salaries exceeding $100,000, laid-off airline pilots, automobile production workers, persons holding advanced degrees, and others whose only *barrier* was the misfortune of not being able to find suitable work.

Employ Your Tax Dollar$ was conceived with two ideas in mind. First, I strongly believe that small and medium-sized business owners deserve to get the same tax advantages and benefits as larger companies when it comes to reducing hiring costs. Workforce development programs prove their worth by getting suitable employment for people who need jobs and by helping businesses meet their hiring needs. Second, providing businesses with E&T program information can help dispel two commonly held myths. One of the myths is that only the poor or low-skilled workers utilize the services of tax supported programs. The other myth is that users of the public workforce system come with a multiplicity of issues that make them undesirable workers.

I want to show business owners how to navigate what may seem to be a complex network of programs to find the workers they need. Relatively low unemployment rates leave small businesses at a competitive disadvantage. By being proactive, business owners can satisfy their hiring needs and their expectations when they engage the services of the E&T agency. This can be a win-win for businesses, for our citizens, and for the workforce development programs mandated to serve both.

Why Should a Business Owner Use Workforce Programs?

Several demographic factors make knowing about workforce development programs important to businesses. Much has been publicized about the anticipated "brain drain" that will occur as a result of the impending retirement of the baby boomer generation. This is not to imply that the generations following aren't as bright. Nothing could be further from the truth! As they've matured, post-boomer generations have had computers, the Internet, cable TV, microwaves, and all the amenities technology can produce. Today's first graders will be employed in jobs that have yet to be created. They will be the backbone of America's economic future in a very short while. I love working with young people who are entering the labor force. I tell them it's important to me that they get good jobs at good salaries because I need them to pay into Social Security so that I can retire comfortably. They usually think I'm joking ... I'm not! In 1950, for every retiree, there were *seventeen Americans at work*. By 1992, the ratio had shrunk to *only three workers for every retiree,* and the gap is steadily closing.[6]

Nevertheless, baby boomers, those who were born in the aftermath of World War II (1946–1964), make up the *largest American generational group*. Approximately 76 million births occurred in America during that period.[7] In 1950, according to US Census records, the birth rate was 24.1 per 1000 citizens. By 1970 the birth rate had declined to 18.4 per 1000. The rate continued to decline and reached 15.5 per thousand in 1983, 84 and 86. Only 1978 saw a lower rate of 15.3. Baby boomer birth rates significantly exceeded the generations that followed.[8] We boomers have had significantly fewer children than our parents had. Therefore, in terms of the *quantity* of workers, shortages are anticipated by 2010, according to source data.[9,10]

Another factor to consider is global competitiveness. In the aftermath of the Cold War, democracy and its cousin, capitalism, were exported around the globe, creating billions of competitors for the world's resources and markets. Our ability to compete will depend on our nation's ability to continue creating the intellectual capital needed to keep the United States on the cutting edge. Our systems for educating and training citizens will either attract or deter other nations from investing in our economy. The cost of labor and the perception that we lack workers skilled in science and technology contribute to driving businesses offshore. The off-shoring of businesses and the use of H1-B visa programs that allow employers to bring skilled workers into the United States are two tools that companies use increasingly because they do not know where to find workers with the skills they need, especially in science and technology.

Larger companies—the Microsofts, IBMs, and AT&Ts of the world—can afford to move entire divisions to India or other countries to save on labor costs. This option is not practical for most smaller companies. Tapping into underutilized human capital sources, such as the people who patronize public workforce development agencies for training and job hunting, can help smaller enterprises to meet their labor needs.

Gaining an intimate knowledge of the E&T system can contribute to significant savings of labor costs and can reduce hiring time while accessing a readily available supply of skilled job seekers. Many people have preconceived ideas about the type of person who utilizes publicly funded agencies. The notion that public agencies only serve "welfare" recipients is misguided (as is the notion that "welfare" recipients can't become excellent employees). During my years of working in Job Training Partnership Act (JTPA) and WIA-funded programs, it wasn't unusual for middle-class workers to state, "I'm not on welfare," or something similar. However, I've counseled and developed training plans for pilots from American, Delta, and United Airlines. Layoffs from General Motors, Hewlett-Packard, Scientific Atlanta, BellSouth, and other corporations brought many a middle-class client to our door. The benefits extended to these highly experienced people while in training were almost identical to the benefits offered to everyone else: free tuition and books, childcare stipends, transportation stipends, career consultation, and planning and other services.

Employ Your Tax Dollar$ is designed to assist businesses to reach the following objectives:

1. **Reduce Costs Associated with Meeting Hiring Needs.** There are more costs than just salary to factor into the price of hiring a new worker. Additional expenses include advertising, screening resumes and applications, interviewing, assessing or testing skills (something that smaller enterprises rarely do), training, and associated learning curves.

2. **Clarify Your Hiring Needs in Terms of Employee Skill Sets, Aptitudes, and Temperaments.** Hiring someone with the wrong skill set or the wrong personality for your company culture is a sure route to employee turnover. I can't overstress the importance of knowing exactly what your business needs in order to prevent a revolving door from becoming a permanent fixture in your business.

3. **Reduce Turnover by Hiring the Best Qualified Person for Your Company**. According to a research study conducted by the Saratoga Institute and Hewitt Associates, the direct costs to replace an employee can be as high as 150 percent of their annual salary.[11]

In business, access to accurate, pertinent information is the key. I intend to inform you about the inner workings of the workforce development field. This can empower you, as a business owner, to recoup a maximum return on the investment you have already made with your tax dollars. You have already paid for the skills that millions of Americans have gained through the public E&T system. You can take advantage of the system's existence and use it to meet your hiring needs, or you can pay a second time to gain a worker for your company. With a greater knowledge of the public system, you can use the entire system, or utilize only those portions of the system that can best meet your business needs. The choice is yours.

1

Put Your Tax Dollars to Work

The 2003 GAO report of E&T programs, in addition to specifying expenditure amounts, also provided the number of participants who used these programs in fiscal years 1999 and 2002. In 2002, 19 million people utilized the Department of Labor's Employment Services. State Departments of Labor are recipients of federal funds that allow them to offer job search assistance to job seekers and labor exchange services to employers. Some services can be accessed over the Internet. Others, for example, registration for Unemployment Insurance Compensation benefits, may require at least one face-to-face interview.

If you go to a Department of Labor office, you can access many services. You can attend a workshop on writing a resume or on preparing for a job interview. If you need to hire a new worker, an account representative will take your job order. Different programs have different funding sources. Veterans see Veterans Representatives who are paid with funds from the Veterans Employment and Training Service. A laid-off worker may get help through the Trade Adjustment Assistance and North American Free Trade Agreement (NAFTA) Traditional Adjustment Assistance programs. A recipient of public assistance may get services from a counselor whose salary is paid through the Food Stamp Employment and Training Program. States are free to design their own programs according to the needs of their citizens. Therefore, Employment Services programs in Georgia may not operate like programs in Pennsylvania, for example.

Learn from the Big Companies

To access E&T services, a business owner must know where to start. They could spend a lot of hours trying to learn which agency can help them get a tax credit, or how they can get a worker's wages subsidized. Large companies don't need to spend time searching for this information because E&T job developers and employment counselors usually contact large employers first. The counselors are required to place large numbers of job-seekers in high-quality jobs. That is done most easily by placing many workers at a single large company. Performance standards for workforce agencies, as set by their funding sources, include meeting placement goals as well as retention goals. It's not just a matter of getting a client a job; the quality of the job is factored in. Are medical benefits provided? Paid vacation and medical leave? Tuition reimbursement? The jobs that include such benefits are labeled "quality jobs." I remember filling out Exit Forms and End of Services screens under the JTPA and WIA programs to report clients who found jobs. Tracking data were entered so that pre-service and post-service factors could be analyzed to determine the impact of the service the client received. Being able to answer these "job-quality" questions in the affirmative is an important success benchmark. Therefore, *job developers and counselors are more likely to seek out partnerships with companies that can place people in quality jobs.* A small-business owner may not be able to offer such an array of benefits and can be easily overlooked.

Carolyn Looff and Associates, under the auspices of the U.S. Small Business Association, published a report called the *Value of Worker Training Programs to Small Business.*[12] The researchers surveyed over a thousand businesses and found that larger firms were more likely to have utilized the E&T system. When the initial study of this subject was done in 1992, 48 percent of employers with fewer than twenty-five employees had heard about the government programs as opposed to 61 percent of those with one hundred or more employees. Seventy-six percent of the largest employers, those with five hundred or more workers, had heard of such programs. By 2001, the numbers in all categories had declined precipitously. The numbers of small businesses (those with fewer than 25 workers) with awareness of these programs—had been cut in half. Even among the largest companies, awareness of the government programs had declined by a significant 30 percent.

In 2001, Carolyn Looff and Associates conducted a follow-up to the 1992 report. Both studies were seeking answers to why government training programs are not being used by businesses. The report offered insights such as that "many do not use them because either they do not know how to go about hiring workers from such programs or because workers from these programs apparently do not know how to find them."[13] The study also drew this conclusion:

> Getting information out to businesses about government training programs and how to use government training programs will be especially useful to the smaller businesses. Not only do they know the least about government train-

ing programs and use them the least, small firms that do not know about or use government programs provide the least training to their workers, and thus could potentially benefit the most from their use.[14]

The Economic Cost of Not Using E&T Programs Can Be High

The implications of such programs for the American economy and the workers that drive it are extremely important. Bear in mind these three important economic factors:

1. **An Impending Worker Shortage.** As I mentioned in the introduction, the United States is facing a worker shortage, due to the "baby bust." American baby boomers, the largest demographic segment, don't have enough children to replace themselves in the workplace. Bureau of Labor Statistics projections estimate that there could be a shortage that will result in millions of skilled positions going unfilled by 2010.[15]

2. **An Impending Skill Shortage.** Not only will we have fewer workers, but we are facing a skill shortage as well. At a time when global markets are expanding and competing for dollars, the number of Americans who won't be able to compete for high-skills jobs grows. Some industries—particularly the sciences, healthcare, and technology—already go begging for workers. Entry-level, low-skill jobs are diminishing; fewer than 20 percent of jobs can be filled by unskilled workers. Nevertheless, our society seems to be generating a surplus of low skilled workers, while the number of low skilled jobs is diminishing.

3. **Under-Utilization of Workers from Certain Demographic Groups**. At the same time, there are groups of citizens that have consistently higher-than-average unemployment rates, despite wanting to work. People with disabilities, older workers (fifty-five and older), African American youth, and persons speaking English as a second language are among these groups. Many of them receive tax-funded assistance when they would prefer to be taxpaying employees.

Bottom line: American workers won't be competitive. We can't grow enough Americans fast enough to meet the demands of the emerging job market. We can import workers from other countries, but many of them will lack even the basic skills needed for entry-level positions. They'll only swell the ranks of the home-grown citizens who themselves lack the skills to qualify for the next generation of jobs. We'll be footing the bill for people who would rather work but can't find suitable jobs that will allow them to make a contribution. This is a distinctively un-American scenario. And, we *can* do better.

The American landscape has changed over generations. Our agricultural society transformed into a manufacturing society. As manufacturing declined, we entered the age of information and technology. This is where we find ourselves today; yet most current job growth is in the service industry. Retail salespersons are at the top of the list of growing jobs through 2012. As the percentage of people employed by companies like General Motors declines, along with their lucrative wages and benefits, they are replaced by people working in companies like Wal-Mart or other retail outlets. A significant portion of the new jobs are part-time and don't provide benefits. Taxpayers are footing the bills for those who lack medical insurance (via Medicaid), or who don't make enough to pay for the basics, including food (via food stamps) and home heating bills (via energy assistance programs).

We know, based on various reports and studies, that most job creation in upcoming decades will be generated by small businesses, not by large corporations. Senator Olympia Snow, Chair of the Committee on Small Business and Enterprise, states: "Small businesses represent 99 percent of all employers, create nearly 75 percent of all net new jobs, and employ 51 percent of the private sector. They are the foundation, the base, the core of our economy. America is America because of our small businesses."[16]

The Small Business Administration (SBA) Office of Advocacy lists several related facts on its Web site:

- Small businesses—defined by the SBA Office of Advocacy as businesses with fewer than five hundred employees—pay more than 45 percent of total U.S. payroll.

- Small businesses generate *between 60 and 80 percent of all new hires in the nation.*

- While there are 17,000 large businesses in the United States, there were *5.8 million small companies with employees.*

- While large firms were cutting 994,667 jobs, small businesses were creating 1,990,326 jobs in 2004, the most recent year for which figures were provided.[17]

In order to help these businesses succeed and expand, wisdom dictates we should provide as much support and assistance as possible to facilitate their access to government programs.

What Services Can A Company Get?

Conceivably, a business can develop a relationship with an E&T agency and get *any kind of assistance they need* as allowed by the agency's governing body and funding source. A multitude of public programs exist to help you meet your hiring needs. Available services include the following:

- Labor exchange services

- Classroom training

- Customized training

- Incumbent worker training

- Tax credits and subsidies

- Apprenticeship programs

- On the job training (OJT)

- Work Experience or Try-Out Employment

- Other services that are creative and unique to a particular locality

Each service has stipulations and requirements that can vary by state or locality. The federal legislation allows a fair degree of local control so that agency boards can determine the needs of their communities and develop their programs accordingly.

Remember, E&T agencies want and *need* to work with your company. Of the forty-four programs listed in the 2002 GAO report on Multiple Employment and Training Programs, thirty-nine of them are judged by their "entered employment" rate—the number of clients getting employment divided by all clients served. Twenty-eight were also judged by their "employment retention" rate, or by how many of their clients were still employed a year later.

Now, before you get excited, remember we are talking about meeting *training and hiring* needs. You can't get the rent on your building paid, or your phone bill, or the note on your company vehicle. You can, however, reap savings in hiring and training, and use the savings to meet your business needs.

E&T Programs Offer Valuable Services

Not all programs are listed under the heading of employment or training. Education programs can also be of great use in meeting employer hiring and training needs. Here's a list of funded programs and their funding source:

- Secondary Vocational Education Programs (Carl D. Perkins Vocational and Technical Education Act)

- Post Vocational Education Programs (Carl D. Perkins Vocational and Technical Education Act)

- Tech-Prep Education (Carl D. Perkins Vocational and Technical Education Act, Title II of Perkins III)

- Employment and Training Activities for Adults, Dislocated Workers, and Youth (Workforce Investment Act, Title I)

- Food Stamp Employment and Training Program (Food Stamp Act)

- Trade Act Programs (Trade Act of 1974, Title II)

- Employment Services (Wagner-Peyser Act)

- Vocational Rehabilitation (Rehabilitation Act of 1973)

- Veterans Programs, including Veterans Employment, Disabled Veterans Outreach Program, and Local Veterans Employment Representative Program (Department of Labor Veterans Employment and Training Service, authorized under Chapters 41 and 42 of Title 38, U.S.C.)

- Temporary Assistance to Needy Families (TANF) (Social Security Act, Part A, Title IV)

- Welfare to Work (Social Security Act, Part A, Title IV)

- Senior Community Service Employment Program (Older Americans Act, Title V)

- Community Development Block Grant Training Activities (Housing and Urban Development)

- Community Services Block Grant Activities (Community Services Block Grant Act)

- Job Corps (Workforce Investment Act)

- Trade Adjustment Assistance (NAFTA)

- Grants to States for Incarcerated Youth Offenders

- Projects with Industry (Rehabilitation Act of 1973)

This is a partial list and doesn't include some programs such as those for Migrant and Seasonal Farm Workers or the Native American Vocational and Technical Education programs. Those programs are specifically designated to assist a small portion of the job-seeking public. Native Americans (including Alaska natives) only comprise 1.5 percent of the U.S. population. Migrant workers represent an equally small segment of the labor force, with the Bureau of Labor Statistics reporting between 900,000 and 1.1 million people employed in this sector.

Employment and Training Programs

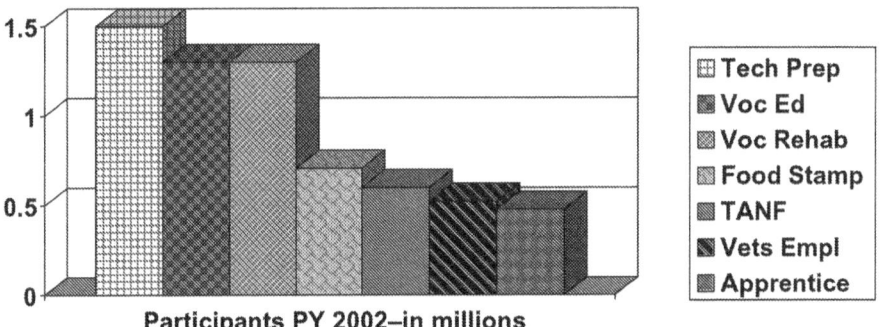

Other than Employment Services (which served 19 million job seekers) and Adult Education, these workforce programs had the highest number of participants in FY 2002 according to the GAO Report of Multiple Employment and Training Programs[18]

The programs listed above aren't restricted to a small qualifying group. They can address the needs of a wide cross section of citizens from the general population.

The Employee You Need Is Being Served by One of These Programs

If we counted the citizens who used the services of all these programs in one fiscal year, (e.g., 2002), the numbers would easily approach the 30-million mark. Conceivably, a student can start accessing these programs while still in high school and continue to receive assistance while in college and after graduating.

For example, Clayton Smith* enrolled in the Summer Employment program each summer following his junior and senior years in high school. He was able to work in the county recreation department as a camp counselor. After graduation, Clayton received a full Pell Grant to cover tuition, books, and expenses associated with attending the local junior college. In addition, he was able to receive a work-study position that allowed him to work twenty hours per week. Prior to graduation, Clayton sought assistance with fees for industry certification in order to begin a career as a medical technician. In total, $12,000 to $15,000 of funds, from several workforce programs, was invested in Clayton's future. Over time, the increased income taxes, property and retail taxes that Clayton will pay will more than replace the taxpayer dollars used to assist him to get a better job.

To obtain optimal benefit from using E&T programs, it is important to know which programs serve which populations. It's just as important to know what kind of employee you need for your business, a factor that is solely within your control, as the owner or human resource manager of the company. When you meet with the E&T representative of a particular program, come with pertinent information regarding your hiring needs—job descriptions, educational requirements, wage levels, other relevant details, and marketing materials. This will give you more credibility than just showing up with "hat in hand." As a potential employer, every business has something it can offer both potential employees and the workforce development agency. If your company can't provide an actual job, it could still offer to be a work-experience site, offer an apprenticeship, or enter into another type of partnership. All parties need to come to the table with something to add to the equation.

*All real client names have been omitted and replaced with pseudonyms.

Services Offered by Public E&T Agencies

Here are descriptions of some of the services offered by public E&T agencies.

- *Labor exchange services* are available to assist job seekers and employers to find each other through posting jobs, interviewing applicants, assessing applicant skills, and making referrals to employers. Depending on the individual office or area, the range of free services can be extensive.

- *Classroom training* serves qualified individuals who need to enter a classroom setting in order to learn marketable skills to get a job. After receiving and completing industry-recognized certification, these clients are available for employment.

- *On-the-job training (OJT)* benefits both a job seeker and a business by allowing funds to subsidize up to 50 percent of the wages of new hires while they are in their training period. The length of the training period will vary according to the position, the skills taught, the qualifications of the new employee, and the speed with which the new employee learns functional tasks. The OJT funds go directly to the employer in the form of a reimbursement as opposed to an up-front grant.

- *Customized training* is similar to OJT in that there is a subsidy of up to 50 percent to cover training costs for a *group* of new workers. The allowable costs, however, don't cover wages. The length of the training is covered in a contractual agreement between the workforce agency and the employer. The workers can be taught in a classroom setting with the instructor, training materials, training space, and other related resources covered by the subsidy. "Customized training" can also refer to any individualized plan of services to a specific company.

- *Apprenticeships* allow an employer to hire an individual and teach him or her a new trade while on the job. The journeyman gets an apprentice who works at an apprentice's wage. The apprentice gets the security of employment at least for the duration of a specified training period appropriate to the trade entered. In addition, the apprentice qualifies for trade or technical school, which may be covered by Pell or other grants. Unlike short-term OJTs, apprenticeships are significantly longer in duration.

- *Work experience* provides opportunities for a business to determine if a client is a good match for the company. Work experience arrangements can be made either with a client who is receiving unemployment insurance compensation due to a layoff, or with a recipient of public assistance. The client works without receiving wages from the employer. The benefit to the business owner is being able to determine whether to hire the client after a specified period of time. The work experience client *may* be paid by the workforce agency, usually at minimum wage. Otherwise, the client may work for free but receive day care, transportation, and/or other assistance.

Another category of assistance to employers includes tax credits or tax subsidies. A tax credit offsets payroll or other taxes related to employee expenses for hiring people with qualifying conditions. Employing veterans, recipients of public assistance, youth, residents of empowerment zones, people with past felony convictions, and older workers can enable a business to qualify for one of the tax credits below.

- Work Opportunity Tax Credit—a federally funded program that reduces tax liabilities associated with hiring new workers with certain qualifying conditions

- Welfare to Work Tax Credit—a federally funded program that reduces tax liabilities associated with hiring long-term recipients of public assistance

- Empowerment Zone/Enterprise Community (EZ/EC) Tax Credits—tax credits obtained by hiring residents in Housing and Urban Development (HUD)–designated EZ/EC areas.

- Retraining Tax Credits—available in some states (Georgia and Virginia, for example) in order to retrain workers on the use of new equipment or technology so that the company can remain competitive. Your local college or Office of Economic Development can provide details about how to take advantage of this kind of tax break if it's available in your state.

You can see from these lists that there are many opportunities for the Employment and Training system to help a small-business owner save much of the time, money, and effort associated with recruiting and retaining his or her workers. The next chapter will focus on the services that are the most utilized and that a business owner can more easily access.

2

Skills Training within Workforce Development Programs

Postsecondary schools, high schools, and colleges receive funds authorized under the Carl Perkins Act or some other tax-supported funding stream. Many of these institutions require that students participate in externships, internships, or unpaid work experiences for academic credit. What better way to give the student a realistic view of the world of work? This also gives an employer the opportunity to nurture and mentor a neophyte professional.

What If You Can't Afford to Pay a Worker?

Unlike programs that involve subsidized wages or tax credits, there usually isn't an eligibility factor involved in internships or work experience arrangements. This can save time by eliminating some of the paperwork separating the participant from the employer. In some fields of study, an internship is mandatory in order to complete requirements for a certificate, diploma, or degree. A teacher or advisor is most likely involved to monitor the progress of the student in the workplace. Some special initiatives are the High School/High Tech Program (HSHT) and the Tech Prep Program.

The High School/High Tech Program is an initiative of the Office of Disability Policy of the U.S. Department of Labor (USDOL). Its focus is to assist "students with all types of disabilities to explore exciting careers in science, mathematics, and technology" according to the USDOL Web site.[19] Work experience activities can consist of site visits, job shadowing, or internships that give a youth firsthand involvement in a real-world setting. In addition to the HS/HT coordinator, students may have a vocational rehabilitation counselor who can purchase adaptive technology if it is needed to enhance the student's workplace performance. They can follow the student's progress and assist the student to increase his or her value to the business. This additional support assures that the employer can focus on teaching work-based skills and provide opportunities to reinforce the work habits taught in the HS/HT curriculum.

Tech Prep is a program funded with Department of Education dollars. Like the HS/HT programs, the focus is on helping students transition from the classroom to the world of work. Starting as early as grade nine, a youth can enroll in a technical education curriculum for four years and transition into a two-year college or approved apprenticeship program. This gives a youth at least four, but possibly six, years of exposure to a technical field, allowing the student to receive industry-recognized certification or a two-year college diploma. My son Keith (yes, that's his real name), who was a Tech Prep student, received a high school diploma with both the Tech Prep and the Academic seals of endorsement, demonstrating that an emphasis on technical skills doesn't have to shortchange academic preparation. As a matter of fact, even more emphasis is placed on academics in order to enhance success in postsecondary ventures. Keith was able to make a smooth transition into technical college without requiring remediation or further preparation.

Internships and work experiences are an important part of the educational process for these students. It's possible for a business owner to find many competent, eager learners who can make a valuable contribution in their workplace.

A Comprehensive Path to Success

Career counseling is a required piece of the Tech Prep curriculum. Students learn about getting and keeping a job, as well as labor market information that helps to point them in a career direction based on their values and aptitudes. Each student's curriculum supports his or her career choice and includes required levels of math, science, language, and vocational skills courses. Once these students have invested a significant period of time preparing for their careers, they are eager for opportunities to join the job market. After performing well in their internships, these students may expect to be hired. If your company hasn't reached that level of profitability, it may be best not to utilize an intern for an extended period of time. You could inform the advisor and the student that your company isn't in a position to hire, but that you would welcome the opportunity to advise and mentor the student. A student could still learn valuable lessons at your company if only for a short period of time. The student would get some exposure to the work world, you would gain a temporary, unpaid employee with a valuable skill set, and the advisor could use the time to help the student find a job that capitalizes on his or her experience.

Vocational education programs and vocational rehabilitation programs also teach occupational skills to their clients. In some instances, collaborative programs allow participants to be the beneficiaries of dual-funding sources. For example, a vocational rehabilitation client may receive training through a Workforce Investment Act (WIA)–funded training provider. They may also have a job coach or counselor from Vocational Rehabilitation (Voc Rehab), and have access to a stipend or work experience wage through a grant-funded program. Such was the case with one young man referred to my office by the administrator of an Office of Disability grant. Our collaboration enabled us to include WIA and Voc Rehab to fund his training and counseling services. The grant was available to fund his supplies and to oversee the process of implementing his career plan, which was to work in the printing industry.

Options beyond Student Interns

The local public assistance agency offers another potential source of unpaid workers. Recipients of Temporary Assistance to Needy Families (TANF) and Food Stamps are held accountable for looking for and finding work. A significant portion of TANF recipients would be considered high-risk employees because they lack a high school diploma, marketable skills, or a prior attachment to the labor market. On the other hand, the only requirement for a family to receive TANF is to have dependent children under eighteen in the home and an income below a certain level.

The story of "Debra Brown" illustrates how a valuable employee can be found among the TANF population. She was a divorced mother of two children and was living with her mother when Debra came to our office to seek assistance with expenses for college. She planned to major in computer programming and was spoken of very highly by her counselor. Since Debra was on TANF, we were able to offer her a work experience position in our office, which allowed her to use the computer skills that she was learning in school. Debra worked with us for more than a year, was very diligent about her duties and attendance, and had good customer service skills. After she graduated with honors, we offered Debra a full-time position with benefits. She is still in that position today. Many "Debras" are on the TANF client rolls and are looking for an opportunity to write their own success stories.

The same is true of many food stamp recipients. A lack of income, not initiative, puts a lot of hard-working people in the food stamp line. They don't want to be there; they long to work and to be restored to their previous social status. The Department of Family Services in your area can give details about the TANF or Food Stamp employment and training programs. The thrust for TANF recipients is to "work first." TANF applicants are required to enroll in a job search program for thirty days. During this time they are able to obtain childcare assistance and other support that can facilitate going to work.

The GoodWorks! program allows recipients to intern at a worksite and maintain their TANF benefits. Upon hiring the recipient, the employer receives the TANF allotment to offset the wages for a specified period of time. After this subsidy ends, the employer can qualify for a Work Opportunities Tax Credit (WOTC) for hiring a worker from one of the qualifying groups. If you are interested in taking advantage of the WOTC opportunity, make sure to submit the recipient's prequalification paperwork prior to putting the recipient on your payroll.

How You Can Get an Experienced Worker

Layoffs are fairly common these days. It doesn't take much for the head of a household to lose a good paying job and find him or herself on the welfare rolls several months later. Work experience opportunities for laid-off workers may be provided through local Departments of Labor. The State of Georgia provides a good example through its GeorgiaWorks Program. Recipients of unemployment insurance compensation are beneficiaries of the coordinated efforts of the Department of Labor, the business community, and the displaced worker.

Michael Thurmond, the Commissioner of Labor, explains the program:

> A laid-off worker identifies a company where they feel they can utilize their existing skills and talents, or learn new ones. This allows the GeorgiaWorks participant to gain a possible hiring advantage. The benefit to the business is the same as in an internship arrangement—a free look at the skills and work behaviors of a possible job candidate. GeorgiaWorks enables businesses to audition potential employees, and it helps the unemployed gain access to training and, potentially, new jobs. What this does is create a transitional period between unemployment and employment.[20]

According to Georgia's DOL Web site, workers are able to get monetary support to defray child care and transportation costs. They can work a maximum of twenty-four hours weekly for up to eight weeks. This is an example of a forward thinking program with win-win-win potential for businesses, for workers, and for workforce organizations.

GeorgiaWorks may be a program unique to Georgia. However, it is easily replicated. Workforce development agencies, particularly Departments of Labor and WIA-funded agencies, are open to suggestions for opportunities to partner with local businesses. Collaboration with a business, an arrangement that can provide child care and transportation support, and a DOL client-referral system can get such an effort underway for the benefit of displaced workers trying to return to work. Dislocated workers, who come from all strata of the labor force from CEOs to janitors to business owners to laborers, are more likely to have a demonstrated work history, which is a requirement to collect unemployment compensation. A good assessment and screening will determine if the worker has the skills, aptitudes, and attitudes that will benefit your business.

3

Make Full Use of Employment and Training Services

Matching the perfect candidate to your company is as much a matter of luck as it is a matter of skill. The one applicant in a thousand who lands the vacant job in your company can consider him-or herself lucky. In the case of labor-exchange services, referring the right candidate is a Department of Labor specialty. Labor Exchange is the most used E&T service by both business and job-seeking clients. In February 2002, the U.S. Department of Labor hosted a "Voice of the Employer" roundtable in Atlanta, Georgia. Thirty-six employers from the Southeast region participated. When asked what services their company obtained from the public E&T system, the services they mentioned most frequently were the labor-exchange functions. Many employers indicated that they use the system as a frequent or primary source for recruiting, screening, testing, and referring employees.[21] Many stated that they participate in Labor Exchange job fairs but no other activities.

Labor Exchange involves gathering job information from businesses, developing job announcements, advertising vacancies, interviewing appropriate candidates, and facilitating referrals so that the employer can interview and hire the candidate of its choosing. Across the United States, this scenario is played out thousands of times on a daily basis; 20 million people used local Department of Labor offices in fiscal year 2002, as reported in the most recent comprehensive Government Accountability Office report. They were primarily involved in some aspect of labor-exchange activities. Your business can save the time and costs associated with advertising; answering calls; responding to faxes, e-mails, or walk-ins; and opening mail; all of which can interrupt business operations for days and disrupt opportunities to generate much-needed revenue.

Labor exchange services allow a business owner to deal only with people who were evaluated and found to have the requirements for the job. An important aspect that many small employers aren't able to handle on their own is a way to *objectively assess* if the candidate has the important qualifications the business requires. The workforce agency can administer skills tests to determine language proficiency, accounting skills, or typing ability, to mention a few possibilities. The cost for these services is not passed on to the employer. What the employer does receive is valuable information regarding a candidate's ability to be productive in the work setting.

The process of matching worker and employer is an important one and can be very basic or very in-depth. In the best interests of all parties, this function is most successful when the business is clear about its needs. Being an expert in your area of service doesn't equate to being an expert in HR activities. It's one thing to say, "I need a receptionist," and quite another to specify, "I need a receptionist with five years' experience operating a multi-line phone, the ability to take messages for four professionals, type forty-five words per minute with 95 percent accuracy, and perform six thousand keystrokes per hour using a ten-key calculator" has a different impact.

How Do You Decide What You Need?

There are ways to go about assessing what you need in order to get a worker who can contribute to your success. Fortunately, there are sources of Labor Market Information (LMI) that can lead you in the right direction. These, too, are publicly funded and paid for with your tax dollars. One resource is the Occupational Network, called O'Net, which can be accessed at http://online.onetcenter.org. O'Net links to http://careeronestop.org, which is easy to navigate and utilize to meet many of your HR needs. You can post job openings, access resumes of job seekers, find tools for writing detailed job descriptions, and review hiring guidelines and policies regarding compliance with wage and hour regulations and workers' compensation. The information found on these Web sites can impact how you go about hiring and training staff for your business.

O'Net is described on its Web page, www.onetcenter.org/hr.htm, as "a free, easy-to-use occupational information system that can help your company save time and effort by leveraging its human resources capabilities [with regard to] challenges in defining job requirements, developing accurate job descriptions, and implementing effective personnel development strategies."[22] Hundreds of job descriptions are available online that can be revised to meet your specific needs. This saves hours of head scratching and assures that the small but important tasks involved in a job aren't overlooked. Information on the O'Net site is readable and written in terms a lay person can easily understand, not in the lingo that sometimes permeates E&T conversations.

In addition, the O'Net site links with other sites that can provide wage information and more pertinent data such as educational requirements. In order to be competitive, it is crucial that a small business offer salaries in line with other businesses. Today's job seekers, especially younger, skilled, better-educated workers, will give little consideration to jobs that offer less than they think they deserve. As well, a small business shouldn't settle for less than "average" requirements to meet their hiring needs. Once a self-assessment is done, taking into consideration your company values, culture, and goals, the job description can be written. The job order can then be submitted to the Employment Service and is the first step in participating in Labor Exchange activities.

In our time-is-money economy, business owners can spend precious time trying to create what they need from scratch, or they can use what their tax dollars have already purchased. As a workforce professional, I frequently advise job seekers to utilize the O'Net site to develop a readable resume for the same reasons that I advocate that businesses use it. The descriptions are thorough, clearly explained, and allow the job seeker and employer to speak a common language.

Workforce agencies, those that are funded by the Workforce Investment Act, also conduct Labor Exchange activities. A plus for WIA agencies is that they have access to individuals who have received occupational skills training. Some job seekers complete the required eligibility process that allows them to receive Individual Training Accounts (ITAs) from WIA-funded agencies. ITAs provide funds that can be used for classroom training from approved schools, including local colleges and technical schools. One of the WIA performance requirements involves credentialing. Trainees who receive industry-recognized certification upon completion are counted towards the agencies' success. These certificates indicate that the trainee has met industry standards and assures that he or she has attained minimum skills.

When a potential employee provides proof of skills certification, then a potential employer can query the agency and candidate about the certification standards. What skills did the trainee learn in order to receive the certificate? What level of proficiency in each skill area must be reached? Does the certification require additional learning or experience in order to be maintained? When does the certification expire? An employee who plans to maintain his or her certification is demonstrating a commitment to his or her profession that suggests the employee will be an invaluable addition to your company. A part of your company's retention practice could involve paying for a course or reimbursing the employee the cost of tuition.

Services Worth the Challenge

Customized training, on-the-job training, and tax credits can be more challenging to take advantage of but can be worthwhile in terms of helping to trim bottom-line personnel costs. Unlike labor-exchange services, hiring workers under these programs requires the new worker to meet program eligibility standards. As a result, there is a paperwork process that involves the employer and the employee. The new employee must meet income, citizenship or immigration status, and Selective Service requirements. There may be additional requirements depending on how the training is funded.

In addition to eligibility for the worker, there will be some type of contractual agreement required of the employer. This may involve pre-and post-hire assessments of the worker's skills to determine that training goals have been met. A detailed job description and an estimate of the number of hours required for the worker to learn the job tasks should be prepared. The assessment can be conducted by the E&T agency or by the employer, as long as an objective process is used.

Some of the language in the contractual paperwork for OJT or customized training will reflect the agency's performance expectations. Your company may be required to provide worker's compensation and to pay into the unemployment insurance compensation fund. There may be a minimum wage requirement, depending on what a "living wage" is considered to be in your area. If it takes a $16,000 annual salary to lift a worker out of poverty, then your offer of a $14,000 yearly salary may not qualify for an OJT subsidy *unless* you develop a career advancement plan that will include pay increases.

You can only hire "eligible" individuals under an OJT contract. Generally, the funding agency determines if the new hire fits its eligibility standards. Eligibility requirements can include compliance with selective service laws as well as proof of citizenship or legal immigration status, residence, or other criteria. There may be a limit on previous earnings levels. Although the employer will not need to determine eligibility, the process can add another step for the potential employee and the employer. Good E&T organizations or their subcontracted service provider will assure that the process doesn't interfere with the company's needs or jeopardize the relationship with you, their business partner.

Some employers view this eligibility process as an attempt to control whom they hire and, in my experience, the process can be a source of some resentment. This is why it's important to use many different hiring avenues to include people from a varied demographic pool. In addition to E&T agencies, local Departments of Labor, schools, colleges, and proprietary institutions have access to individuals who can meet the eligibility standards set by local boards. Completion of the eligibility process and approval of the OJT position must be done prior to the start of the first day on the job. Since the sponsoring workforce agency reimburses only a part of the training wage, and does not reimburse once the training period ends, a business must be able to meet its payroll responsibilities without the subsidy. For this reason, new companies may find it difficult to get an OJT approved.

A business using on-the-job training may save thousands of dollars. For example, if the OJT pays $10 per hour ($400/week) and lasts twelve weeks ($4800), and the agreement calls for a 50 percent reimbursement, a $2400 savings can be realized. In some instances, the E&T agency may have a payment scale that reimburses a set amount as opposed to a percentage.

In the case of group training such as under a customized training model, a training curriculum may be required. Often business owners, especially of smaller enterprises, have difficulty negotiating the paperwork process involved in a customized training arrangement. The language of the contract can be challenging to understand and complete. The contract will stipulate the terms, including the start and ending dates, a statement of work, the number of funded participants, the amount of the contract, and other legal conditions that the business must meet. Many E&T agencies handle the paperwork process for the employer. Nevertheless, these are legal documents complete with legal jargon and E&T terminology. As a business owner, you should probably obtain legal advice.

Customized training is provided for an employer or group of employers who have committed to hire individuals who successfully complete the training. The workforce development agency will determine if the training is in an area of occupational demand (e.g., health care, technology, auto repair). Not only do some fields face shortages, there are some jobs for which it is hard to recruit and retain workers. Examples are credit account representatives (bill collectors), retail sales clerks and call center workers. Labor market information for your area can show the employment figures and verify the need. Once completed, recruitment of eligible trainees can proceed. A business can get reimbursement of up to 50 percent of the training costs associated with customized training.

A small-business owner can be overwhelmed by how much involvement this takes. The funding source may have staff available to assist with the paperwork, but it still requires the employer to bring something to the negotiating table. Most small-business owners are skilled professionals who are good at running their businesses. This type of hiring, however, takes them into uncharted waters.

I remember working with a small employer who wanted to expand his business and hire several drivers for a transportation company. Because the business only involved the owner and a secretary, they were unable to attend meetings, develop a curriculum, write job descriptions, or submit wage data and other pertinent information. There were things that our agency couldn't do for them, and that they didn't have the time or skills to do for themselves.

This event was a catalyst for creating my *Employ Your Tax Dollar$* workshop. I began to understand that this scenario was playing out in large numbers of small businesses on a daily basis. The implications for the agency where I worked, and for the nation, was that jobs were being lost, citizens were remaining unemployed, potential company profits went unrealized, and taxes and other revenue weren't being contributed to the local economy.

It is worth using OJT and customized training arrangements, even though they can be complex and time-consuming. Unlike the generic training that people receive in classroom settings, OJT and customized training result in your company getting an employee whose training is tailored for your business—no one else's. Remember, you have to train the worker anyway. Why not get a financial break for doing so?

Apprenticeship Programs Have Retention Benefits

Apprenticeship training is a nationally recognized method of training new workers. As a matter of fact, apprenticeships have been used for centuries to impart valuable skills training to young workers in trades such as blacksmithing. The New York State Department of Labor Web site describes its apprenticeship programs as "a method which combines actual work experience with classroom related instruction and produces a worker skilled in the occupation who is capable of exercising independent judgment and who subscribes to the highest standards of professional conduct."[23]

The stipulations for participation on both the part of the employer and the apprentice are set forth in a contractual agreement, and the apprenticeship program and curriculum must be approved. Many apprenticeship programs may be under the aegis of a union or worker association such as the International Brotherhood of Electrical Workers, and have a curriculum that is standardized by the related industry. Depending on the skills and the occupational area, apprenticeships can last anywhere from one to six years. A master journeyman is responsible for sponsoring the apprentice during that time. Essentially, an apprentice who performs satisfactorily in both the classroom and the job setting is guaranteed a job during the apprentice period.

Many apprenticeships are clustered in the trade areas, but they can also be created in positions involving specific job skills. The North Carolina Department of Labor's Web site has a nineteen-page listing of apprenticeable positions and the number of training hours required to complete and receive industry certification. The number of apprentices entering many trades is not keeping pace with the number of journeymen who are retiring. There is great demand for electricians, plumbers, carpenters, welders, and others. However, the types of occupations that can utilize apprenticeships as a learning tool are not limited to trade occupations.

The Office of Apprenticeships of the USDOL Employment and Training Administration has guidelines and provides technical assistance for employers and employer groups who are interested in establishing apprenticeship programs. They can help with creating the curriculum, understanding the worksite requirements, and defining other standards appropriate for your industry. Consult the Office of Apprenticeship, the State Apprenticeship Council, or another recognized agency in your state for more information.

Workers hired under an apprenticeship arrangement can make a valuable addition to your business. By the nature of the arrangement, a worker who participates indicates a willingness to make a commitment to learning as well as a commitment to the company. These are important qualities from which all employers would benefit.

Tax Credits—A Different Kind of Benefit

Employers can obtain tax credits by hiring people who fit into a category that has been labeled "hard to serve." The E&T agency won't speak with the employer about people who are "hard to serve" or who have "barriers to employment." This is E&T industry lingo. But be aware (notice I didn't say beware!) that people who generate a tax credit when they are hired will fall into one of the qualifying categories, which are:

• Recipients of public assistance (Temporary Assistance to Needy Families)

- Food Stamp recipients

- Persons with disabilities

- Recipients of Supplemental Security Income

- Ex-offenders who have committed a felony

- Qualified veterans

- High-risk youth

- Youth who meet particular qualifications for summer employment

The "hard to serve" label can be a misnomer because it implies that people who fit this category are more difficult to deal with. This isn't always the case any more than it would be for people who don't fit into "hard to serve" groups. What is hard, many times, is finding the resources that enable people to rise above their circumstances. Harder still is finding business owners who are willing to take the risk and employ an ex-offender, a person with a disability, an older worker, an immigrant who lacks English proficiency, or a welfare recipient. Youth from poorer backgrounds are at higher risk for drug abuse, getting into the criminal system and other social maladies. Economic data validates that people who fit these descriptions have unemployment rates higher than those of the general population. Consequently, tax credits are available for employers to offset the costs associated with hiring these workers.

The caveat of receiving a tax credit is that you should determine whether the new hire fits the qualifying category before extending an offer of employment. IRS Form 8850, Pre-Screening Notice, can be used for this purpose. Once you make a determination, submit the required documentation to the appropriate agency, which will probably be your state's Department of Labor. When certification of eligibility is provided, you will be able to claim the tax credit on your business tax return.

There is a $2400 maximum credit that can only be applied to a worker who is employed with your business at least 120 hours. If the employee was hired under a subsidized program such as an OJT, no credit can be claimed for the wages earned *during the period covered by the subsidized program*. However, the credit can apply to subsequent wages. It is possible to hire a qualified worker under a wage subsidized program like OJT and get additional financial savings via a tax credit for the same worker. Your business can realize significant savings on a salary and use it for worker incentives such as tuition reimbursement, or you can put it back into the business in other ways.

Here's an illustration of how your business might benefit from a workforce development program subsidy.

A small law office needs a legal assistant and paralegal. The job description reads:

> Full-time position, $25,000 to $30,000 salary, depending upon experience, high school graduate, prior legal experience in a law office desirable but not required. Need assistant with secretarial skills for typing, filing, answering phones, making client appointments, and other related duties for a two-lawyer office. Requires good interpersonal skills.

An administrative assistant with no prior paralegal experience may take forty business days, or eight weeks, to become proficient in using legal terms, preparing legal documents, conducting legal research, and other tasks.

Pre-OJT assessment shows that the new employee types sixty words per minute and is proficient in MS Word, Access, and Excel programs. The on-the-job training would involve learning legal terms, how to prepare legal documents such as affidavits and contracts, and how to use a legal library to conduct research. The starting OJT salary of $12 per hour would be subsidized at 50 percent. Calculate the wage reimbursement as follows:

$$8 \text{ hours/day for 40 days x } 12/\text{hour} = \$3,840.$$
$$\$3,840 \text{ divided by 50 percent} = \$1,920.$$

The business saves $1,920 on the cost of the paralegal's salary for the eight-week OJT period. Upon successful completion of the OJT, the employee would receive a raise. The savings gained from the OJT would pay for the raise for the next five months or so.

Prior to hiring the worker, the employer determines that the worker is a member of a targeted group and has the worker certified as such. (See IRS form 8850). The employer then becomes eligible for a tax credit of *up to* $2,400. The tax credit would apply after the OJT subsidy ends.

I would advise any business interested in taking advantage of tax credits to hire a tax professional in order to assure that the tax forms are filled out correctly. The instructions accompanying these forms indicate varying time frames to learn about the law, prepare the forms, and file them accordingly.

Form 8826—Disabled Tax Credit (93 minutes)
Form 5884—Work Opportunities Tax Credit (2 hrs, 9 minutes)
Form 8861—Welfare to Work Tax Credit (3 hrs, 23 minutes)

These time estimates don't include collecting the necessary documentation, which is a crucial part of any tax-related activity. At the very least, utilize knowledgeable professionals to conduct pre-screening activities until you are comfortable doing so. Your local Department of Labor or Department of Revenue office can be of great assistance.

Can Your Business Afford to Use These Services?

To be honest, you may realize that your business is not at the stage where it can afford to participate in anything beyond the labor-exchange activities offered by the local DOL agency. That's okay. The word *free* implies that no costs are associated with some of the services. At the very least, it will cost time to put in a job order, not to mention transportation expenses, and the time that you or one of your employees spends participating in job fairs. The wages, costs of training, and other employee expenses associated with customized and OJT activities must be spent up front. It may take thirty days or more to receive reimbursement. A tax credit takes even longer. Realistically, your business will still have to remain solvent, pay expenses, keep the doors open, and generate enough money to pay yourself and your new employee. The worksheet located in the appendix can be used to figure out what the financial impact would be for hiring people under a reimbursement contract, such as on OJT. There are no hard and fast rules to follow, so you can decide how much of your net revenue you want to dedicate to a wage reimbursement program.

4

Get the Best Workers for Your Business

○ ○
Many job seekers are available in the service stream of workforce agencies; assess thoroughly and choose selectively in order to get the best workers for your business

One practice employed regularly in workforce development agencies is conducting assessments. Over 85 percent of the customers who utilized Employment and Training services in 2002 received some type of assessment, according to the GAO report.[24] An assessment consists of both objective and subjective measurements of an individual's skills and workplace readiness. Once you've provided information regarding your preferences, the E&T agency can screen candidates based on your specifications. Assessment instruments fall into these categories: interests, aptitudes, personality, skills, achievement, and job readiness. Some are hybrids and measure more than one area, such as interests *and* aptitudes.

People Get Nervous About Taking Tests

Some kinds of assessment instruments aren't considered "tests" since there are no "right" or "wrong" answers. Examples of interest inventories are the O'Net Interest Profiler or the Holland's Self-Directed Search. Both can be self-administered and are based on the Holland Codes popularized by John Holland, author of the best seller *What Color Is Your Parachute?* In the O'Net interest inventory, respondents must decide if they "like," "don't like," or "have no opinion" of a task like "Build kitchen cabinets." The answers to the inventory questions are grouped into categories: realistic, artistic, investigative, social, enterprising, and conventional. The top three interest areas are matched to jobs and/or careers that the respondent may find satisfaction in performing. For example, a file clerk or truck driver is in the conventional category, a teacher or nurse aide in the social category. A job seeker can complete the instrument, score the responses, and interpret the answers on his or her own.

Workforce development counselors and professionals are able to administer and interpret a variety of assessment instruments. Sometimes assessment instruments form the basis for a workshop in which all of the attendees answer the questions together and the interpretation is done by the workshop facilitator. Either method is valid, but entry-level workers or others who aren't used to taking "tests" benefit most from a facilitator's help. The purpose of these types of inventories is to help job seekers clarify what they would like to do in a job setting. An individual who wants to "work with people" may not find satisfaction in a job where handling paperwork is the primary task. Also, liking to do a particular job is an internal motivator that drives people to hang in there even when the job isn't what they would consider their ideal job.

If you would like to get a feel for taking an interest inventory, many are available on the Internet. Often the testing is free, as in the case of the Jung Typology Test (www.humanmetrics.com) or the Motivational Appraisal of Personal Potential (www.assessment.com), and a brief explanation of the results is provided. For a fee, the results can be thoroughly analyzed.

Aptitude inventories are objective ways of measuring a job seeker's potential to learn skills, or the degree to which the job seeker has the ability to perform in some specific areas. Verbal, numerical, mechanical, and abstract reasoning, spatial aptitude, and manual dexterity are some areas that can be measured. Aptitude tests usually are more expensive than interest inventories. The Differential Aptitude Test (DAT) and the Career Scope fall into this category. The Career Scope costs from $3,000 to over $50,000 dollars to purchase and would allow multiple applicants to be tested. It also includes an interest component that can be used in combination with the aptitude results to get a comprehensive picture of the client's abilities.

Aptitude tests may take longer to administer and must be interpreted by a trained professional. Results are reported in terms of "percentile ranks," stanines (a nine point scale creating a bell curve), and/or grade equivalents, which an untrained administrator may find difficult to interpret. There are time factors to take into consideration since many scores are rated based on how many items were correctly answered during a specified period of time. Another aspect to be considered is the reading level of the instrument. Inventories like the Differential

Aptitude Test, an eight-test battery, have a seventh grade reading level and shouldn't be given to people unable to read at that level. The Career Scope can be administered to readers at the fourth grade level and can be adapted for people with disabilities as well.

Achievement tests measure a person's level of skill in a given area or areas. The most common achievement tests are used to measure reading and math skills, which are generally reported in terms of grade level. The Tests of Adult Basic Education (TABE) and the Wide Range Achievement Tests (WRAT) are fairly common. The TABE is a diagnostic instrument that has both a short and a long version. Another plus is that the test can be purchased at different levels of difficulty depending on the population to be tested. School-age children can be given the Easy (level E) test. Adults who want to enter into advanced training or who are seeking a job that requires a high school diploma or college degree can be administered a Difficult (level D) or Advanced (level A) instrument. It isn't unusual for a group of clients to be in the same room taking varied levels of the TABE, which is timed the same across the different levels.

The simplicity or complexity of a job determines the level of reading or math proficiency that's needed. Reading, writing, mathematics, listening, and speaking comprise the list of basic or foundation skills recognized by the 1990's Secretary's (of Labor) Commission on Achieving Necessary Skills (SCANS) report. *There is no job in the world that doesn't utilize some combination of these skills.* You may need to determine if your new employee can find, understand, and interpret printed information (in other words, how good your employee's reading skills are). You should require an objective measurement of the worker's ability to read. Generic reading may be all that is required, or an employee may need to be skilled at reading industry-specific terms, definitions, and instructions. Can your potential worker communicate in writing? How well does he or she spell? Does he or she use correct grammar? How do you want the employee to demonstrate this ability? Does your employee need to perform calculations or estimations? Perform measurements? How about reading a diagram or a graph? There are tests that can be instrumental in providing some of the information you'll want to consider in judging a person's suitability for your job. The impact on worker productivity makes basic skill levels relevant information to obtain.

People *Should* Go Through All This to Get Your Job

When used properly, assessments can be an important part of the screening process for new employees. Businesses like BellSouth, for example, regularly test aptitudes when they are looking to hire technical workers. Some people think that tests are biased and make it difficult for a person to perform well. However, many types of tests allow some flexibility, in timing or administration, so that everyone has the opportunity to perform their best. Another benefit that can be extended to people with special needs is to use adaptive equipment. Departments of Labor and WIA-funded centers have adaptive equipment that makes reading easier, or that can read a test instrument to clients who have visual impairments.

Test results can be very accurate when the instruments are used according to the publisher's guidelines and administered well. I remember a client, "Mr. Jones," who took a test that revealed his spatial skills ranked in a low percentile range. This caused some concern regarding his request to obtain a commercial driver's license. His counselor knew that spatial skills were crucial for successfully handling a vehicle, like an eighteen-wheel truck, that a driver can't see around. Nevertheless, WIA has a principle of customer choice, and we (reluctantly, I'll add) allowed "Mr. Jones" to exercise his choice. He did well, even completed the training, and got a job. He kept the job until ... he backed the truck up into a fence at work and got fired!

We can't allow the inventories or tests to tell the whole story. E&T professionals know how to assess the hard data of test results (reading levels, keystrokes per minute, spelling score, etc.) and also to interpret what the intangibles reveal. When a client is interviewed, more than just asking and answering questions is involved. Observation, active listening, "Socractic" questioning techniques, and interpretation skills are utilized. Gaps in answers and inconsistencies can be addressed, but beyond just addressing the inconsistencies, good counseling can teach a client how to deal with issues in an honest, positive manner to the benefit of the client and the client's future employer. Once people who meet your qualifications have been referred to you, you can conduct an interview to determine which job seeker you want for the job.

In using labor exchange services, you can limit the number of people referred to any position you advertise. State what skills you want a worker to have and request objective testing that can validate your requirements. Include what you feel are the most important interest areas for the job. Ask what, if any, interest inventory was administered. Some agencies can conduct a more extensive assessment than others. Interview the representative of the agency, just as you do any other professional whose services you engage, to determine the steps they will undertake to help you find the best person for your company. If the agency can't perform the testing, they can collaborate with a partner on your behalf to get the testing done. The caveat: the partner agency may only administer some types of tests to "eligible" candidates. Therefore, a step to determine eligibility may be included and lengthen the process as a result.

Thorough Screening Is Important

According to the Association of Certified Fraud Examiners, "46 percent of all workplace fraud occurs at companies with fewer than one hundred employees."[25] The first fraudulent act that many job seekers commit is putting false information on their resumes or applications. The same article cites a 70 percent occurrence rate. Agencies may conduct background checks as one of the services they offer to their business customers. You may find that they'll conduct drug tests as well. WIA-funded training may require candidates for training to submit to a drug test. Ask if such testing is a part of the local policy. Local Departments of Labor can get potential employees bonded to offset the potential losses of theft or fraud, especially if the job seeker has been convicted of committing a felony offense. You should inquire about what, if any, background documentation has been gathered on a potential new hire who has been referred. The agencies are prepared to share information, within the parameters of the law, and can have their clients sign an agreement giving permission to do so.

Remember, the public E&T system wants and needs to work with you, the business partner. These partnerships are of ultimate importance to the success of the system and the people they serve. Not only do they need and want your business, they also want your respect. I have had the opportunity to work and network with hundreds of E&T professionals from all over the nation. Their top concern is customer satisfaction, and business is their number one customer!

5

Develop and Keep Qualified Workers

In these competitive times, where getting and keeping the best workers remains challenging, a business can and should use all the help available to prevent employees from walking out the door, taking their skills and knowledge with them.

There are some valid reasons why employees leave. In more than a few instances, they get fired, and with good cause. Admittedly, there are some people who don't really want to work. Who doesn't like free money? If an employee can show up, do nothing, and still get paid—well, why not? That's the attitude many workers seem to have. "They should be glad I showed up" may not be expressed in words as much as in behavior. You know the issues: chronic tardiness, frequent absences, personal problems that interfere with job performance, and so on. A small-business owner once told me that the biggest challenge he faced was the inability to recruit and retain "good" workers.

In E&T jargon, we refer to "job readiness." There are workshops and programs dedicated to teaching workers how to get to the job on time, how to organize their personal lives, how to prioritize, how to juggle responsibilities, how to learn accountability. You see, we can't take it for granted that everyone has these "soft" skills. And if we start talking about attitudes, that would be a separate chapter. Not everyone in our society buys into the concept of "work" as most of us define it. One thing that good job readiness programs explore is the participant's motivation regarding going to work. Is there someone at home prodding a family member to "get a job"? Is there a probation officer or a "baby momma" somewhere in the background? External motivators, like money, can be effective initially. The participant will accept a job, but will he or she come to work every day, show up on time, and have a good attitude? Not likely.

Sometimes Good Ones Leave, Too

As for the others—the ones with good attitudes, good skills, and a desire to work—why do they leave? The list can include factors that the best boss can't control. The job commute is one example. It's no one's fault if a job commute takes an hour over a crowded highway. In places like Atlanta, commutes can be brutal if you live in one of the outlying suburbs and work in the city. I was fortunate to live about seven miles away from my job for most of my career. Despite the fact that my job was literally down the street, over the years, as the population grew and cars clogged the roads, my fifteen-minute drive turned into a forty-five-minute commute. Even at that, my story is rare in a town where two-hour commutes, *one way*, aren't unheard of. Atlanta has a collection of highways that rivals those infamous highways in Los Angeles. As a matter of fact, Atlanta and L.A. compete for first place in longest commute times. Unlike New York, Philadelphia, or D.C., public transportation isn't as flexible, and you need a car to get to where the jobs are. In order to endure this kind of punishing commute, you'd want top compensation in wages, benefits, and job satisfaction. Otherwise, the job may not seem worth the impact on the quality of life.

Good workers may leave if the job isn't challenging or doesn't use their strongest skill sets. Maybe there's no advancement in their foreseeable future. When I relocated to the Atlanta area, my first professional position was as an intake worker which primarily involved clerical tasks. After a couple of years of filling out forms, making copies of documents, and doing eligibility interviews, I was on the road to serious burnout and decided to quit. When I confided in a program manager, he promptly reported the conversation to the agency director. Fortunately for me, the director offered me another position. Although it was a lateral move, it involved more decision making, independent work, creativity, and flexibility. My positions continued to evolve until I became a program manager, a position that allowed me to advance my skills to the point that I could retire relatively early, and start my own consulting and training company.

It's important not to hire workers who have higher-level skill sets than you need. If you need a cashier, don't hire an accountant no matter how impressive he or she is. Unemployed people sometimes lament that they "can't even get a job at McDonald's." The reality is that they wouldn't be happy even if they could! Who would want to supervise the former computer programmer whose day is now an endless stream of "Would you like fries with that?"

A worker may divorce himself or herself from the company because he or she doesn't feel the salary is adequate. Often, smaller businesses aren't able to compete with larger companies in terms of their compensation packages. Interview your job candidates thoroughly. Ask about their past experiences and motivation for wanting to work in *your* business. Their responses may help you to choose the worker who can find career satisfaction there.

Workforce development programs can assist in your retention efforts from the recruiting stages through the probation period by carefully screening and assessing potential employees and by helping you to offer retention incentives. Some of their programs' clients may qualify for assistance with their child care and/or transportation expenses or other "supportive services." One example is the transitional benefits provided to recipients of public assistance. A TANF recipient who goes to work full-time can receive free childcare subsidies for an entire year. This can go a long way toward relieving some of the financial responsibility associated with going to work.

Lack of affordable child care is one disincentive that parents speak of when considering taking a job. It's not just about getting a job. Many times, it's not even the job itself, but other things that accompany going to work. Just as there are business owners who don't know that they can gain a tax credit for hiring workers with certain characteristics, some workers may not know that they can qualify for child care tax credits or an Earned Income Tax Credit (EITC). Every paycheck can reflect a tax break if the worker knows how to get it. Making this happen for a new employee provides one more reason for him or her to keep coming back every day. As your employee continues on the job, you will want to inquire of the local Department of Labor office regarding any training incentives for employers. There may be a way to get free "incumbent worker" training, depending on what field your business is in. If it's a field that's in demand, or one in which jobs are being lost, such as manufacturing, your DOL agency may have funding to reduce the potential loss of jobs. A worker in an entry-level position may still qualify for WIA-funded training programs. Some training providers are flexible and run classes on the weekend, during the evenings, or online.

As a part of your initial discussion with a new employee, you should become involved in developing a career plan for him or her with your company. This would include a discussion of where the employee wants to be in a year, or two years, or five. It's not that either of you will be able to predict the future; however, making the plan creates a blueprint that can be used to develop the worker's potential. As your business grows, your employee can grow to the benefit of all concerned. A worker is more willing to stay with, and do a good job for, a company that has his or her benefit at heart.

One of my best friends started working for a company that was run by a husband and wife team out of an office in the back of their home. She didn't have related experience but was offered the job nevertheless. One of the reasons she took the job, despite the low pay, was that the couple had a swimming pool and were pleased to let her use it at lunchtime and after work. Twenty years later, she's still with the company. As the company grew and the revenue increased, she received profit-sharing checks, stock options, paid training and conferences. The owners are selling the business this year. My friend will be able to leave the company with a large financial compensation package. None of this was foreseeable at the time but came to fruition as a result of the couple's good business management and desire to keep a good worker.

Few people want to stay in a dead-end job. If you don't *plan* to keep the worker, then don't expect to. If you don't mind a revolving-door policy for your company, then so be it. Just keep in mind that your $8-an-hour worker can cost you as much as $12 an hour to replace. It's like an old song says, "It's cheaper to keep her" than let her walk out the door and take your investment of time, training, mentoring, and knowledge with her.

The incentive is not just to the workforce agency but to the community and state in which the business is located. Job creation and job retention means revenue and income production. Economic development and workforce development are inextricably bound in a way that can ensure the success or failure of a community. It's in everyone's interest to support an employer's efforts to keep workers skilled and competitive and participating in the success of the economic development of our society and its communities.

6

Ensure the Economic Future of Our Communities

Let's imagine a scenario where everyone who wants to work is employed in the job of their choice. Let's also imagine that each worker is making enough in wages and benefits that the number of people receiving public assistance, food stamps, SSI, and other entitlements drops precipitously. To expand on the fantasy, let's envision an increase in savings and a decrease in personal and national debt levels.

What would American society be like? Might our public discourse change from "How are we going to fund entitlement programs?" to "How should we invest the budget surplus?" Would people be less stressed? Would there be less crime? Would families spend more time together?

I don't have all the answers. Nor can I truthfully say, much as I'd like to, that using the workforce development system will result in such a lofty vision. I can say with certainty that our tax dollars provide services to some citizens who could otherwise be overlooked. Some citizens are undervalued and others are overworked. We can't fix everything. A job isn't the answer to all our woes. But we can change *some* things. The good part of the equation is that everybody can find themselves on the winning side. A win for business, a win for job seekers, and a win for workforce organizations is possible every time a business uses workforce services.

Not to stand on the soap box too long, I'll close by adding that I love the workforce development profession. It goes back to the old adage that we've heard all of our lives about teaching a man to fish. Think about the challenge of fishing. Sometimes it's exciting; other times it's boring. Sometimes the waters are calm and clear; sometimes they are choppy and turbulent. Then you catch a big one. It's a moment of pride, of satisfaction, and of accomplishment. You don't just smile, you grin—widely. I believe people should have that same feeling at the end of a good day's work and surely on payday.

You see, in America, we are our work. Maybe it shouldn't be this way; maybe one day it'll change. But, for the moment, we must admit that after we find out a stranger's name, the next question we frequently ask is "What do you do"? Our work is how we explain our reason for being. Identity, status, and value are all encompassed in the work we do with our hands, our backs, and our brains.

There is room for everyone in the world of work. Some people work part-time, some work full-time, some are on flex schedules, some work on contract. American society needs everyone who is capable of making a contribution to do so if we are going to be competitive. That's where *you* come in. I pray that your business makes you prosperous, whatever you define prosperity to be. That you, and I, will "prosper and be in good health even as our souls prosper" is my prayer. Small businesses are at the forefront of national prosperity and economic development. The nation will follow where we lead. We create the jobs. We create the ideas. We provide the economic energy that this nation requires in order to be healthy. We are all paying for some powerful tools that can help us in our ventures. Let's pay it forward. Our children and our children's children will thank us.

You have already paid for the services that will help you save time, money, and effort. The workforce development system can help you become more competitive in the global marketplace by providing you access to a diverse pool of human capital. Whenever you can, however you can, for as many as you can, you should Employ Your Tax Dollar$.

APPENDIX A

Subsidized Cost Reimbursement Worksheet

☐ On-the-Job Training   ☐ Customized Training
☐ Apprenticeship   ☐ Tax Credit

Employee
Hourly Wage: $_____ x _____ Hrs/Wk x _____
Weeks = $_____

◆   ◆   ◆

BALANCE SHEET*

1. Monthly Revenue

a.	Accounts Receivable	$_____
b.	Other income	$_____
c.	Other income	$_____

2. Total Revenue	$_____

3. Monthly Expenditures

a.	Rent/Mortgage	$_____
b.	Utilities	$_____
c.	Insurance	$_____
d.	Office Supplies	$_____
e.	Equipment	$_____
f.	Other	$_____
g.	Other	$_____
h.	Other	$_____

4. Total Expenses	$_____

5. Net Revenue	$_____

6. Employee Wage/Net Revenue	_____%

Calculations

OJT: Wage total x .50 or other reimbursement percentage

Apprenticeship: Weekly salary x number of weeks

Tax credit: Deduction varies and is based on the length of the employee's tenure. $750.00, $1.200.00, or $2,400.00

* Note: This list does not include all the expenses that may be involved in running your business. Different kinds of business incur different types of expenses. The more inclusive the better, so as to more accurately reflect to what extent a tax credit or wage subsidy may impact business revenue.

APPENDIX B

A list of tax-sponsored programs by special population served.

Benefit to Business	Tax Credit	Wage Subsidy	Program Administrator or Service Provider
Adults: 18+			
Up to 50% of new hire training costs	—	• WIA-OJT • WIA Customized Training	• Local Workforce Boards
Up to $500 credit for a f/t employee	Employer Retraining Tax Credit	—	State Department of Revenue (GA and VA only)
Up to $2400 credit for hiring SSI/Voc Rehab Recipients	Work Opportunities Tax Credit	—	State Office of Vocational Rehabilitation Services

Youth: 16–21			
Wages offset for summer jobs May 1 through Sept. 15	Work Opportunities Tax Credit	—	State Departments of Labor
Wages offset or subsidized for businesses in designated areas	Empowerment Zone Tax Credits	Summer Employment	Local Workforce Boards
Laid-Off Workers			
Work Experience		Part-time, try-out employment	Local Departments of Labor
Veterans			
Up to $2400 tax credit	Work Opportunities Tax Credit	—	Veterans Administration
Up to 50% of new hire training costs	—	WIA-OJT WIA Customized Training	Local Workforce Boards

TANF Recipients			
Federal tax credit up to $3500 for 1ˢᵗ year	Welfare to Work Tax Credit	—	State Department of Labor
Wage subsidy = up to 9 months TANF grant	—	TANF Subsidized Employment	Local Department of Welfare
Federal credit *Up to $2400 per new hire*	Work Opportunities Tax Credit	—	• State Office of Vocational Rehabilitation Services • Internal Revenue Service
Up to 50% of new hire training costs	—	WIA-OJT WIA Customized Training	• Local Workforce Boards
People with Disabilities			
Job Coaching, purchasing assistive technology for a person with a disability	Disabled Access Credit	—	• State Office of Vocational Rehabilitation • Internal Revenue Service

Refugees			
Work Experience—temporary employment at no cost to the employer	Food Stamp Employment Program	—	• Local TANF agencies • Local Workforce Investment Boards

Older Workers (55+)			
Work experience—agency paid temporary employment	—	Senior Community Service Employment Program	Local subgrantees of the Department of Labor

Endnotes

1. The definition of what constitutes a small or medium-sized business varies. For this publication, a small business shall refer to a business with 50 or fewer employees.

2. *Value of Worker Training Programs to Small Business*, prepared for the Small Business Association, Carolyn Looff and Associates, September 27, 2001

3. *Employers Are Aware of, Using, and Satisfied with One-Stop Services, but More Data Could Help Labor Better Address Employers' Needs*, United States General Accounting Office, GAO-05-259, February 2005. The full report, GAO-05-259, which includes the scope and methodology of the study, can be found on the GAO Web site.

4. *Multiple Employment and Training Programs, Funding and Performance Measures for Major Programs*, United States Government Accounting Office, GAO-03-589, April 2003.

5. HRMS Net Assets, www.hrms-netassets.net, August 25, 2004.

6. CRS Report for Congress (94-27) Social Security: Brief Facts and Statistics, May 1998.

7. Baby Boomer Headquarters, www.bbhq.com, November 21, 1006.

8. U.S. Census Bureau, Statistical Abstract of the United States: 2007, Table 76. Live Births, Deaths, Marriages and Divorces: 1950 to 2004.

9. For American Business, A New World of Workers, Business Week, September 19, 1988, Pages 112–19

10. Despite Expected Labor Shortages, Few Employers Are Seeking Older Workers, http://mckover.newsedge.com, August 18, 2003.

11. NAWDP Advantage, National Association of Workforce Development Professionals Newsletter, December 2005, Vol. 18 No. 12.

12. Looff and Associates, Page v.

13. Looff and Associates, Page v.

14. Looff and Associates, Page vi.

15. The Hunt for Talent, Jon Roberts, TIPS Strategies July, 2006

16. Senator Olympia Snow, "Committee on Small Business and Entrepreneurship", www.sba.gov.

17. Frequently Asked Questions (SBA Office of Advocacy), June, 2006.

18. Graph represents figures from GAO-03-589, Appendix IV: Estimated Number of Program Participants Who Received Employment and Training Services, Page 24.

19. www.dol.gov/odep. U.S. Department of Labor, Office of Disability Employment Programs, High School High Tech Program, 1/03/2007

20. www.dol.state.ga.us/spotlight/sp georgia works.htm. Georgia Department of Labor, GeorgiaWorks, 1/3/2007

21. "Voice of the Employer" Summary of Results, U.S. Department of Labor, February 19, 2002, Page 2

22. www.onetcenter.org/hr.html. Occupational Information Network Resource Center, Human Resources Management. 1/3/2007

23. www.labor.state.ny.us/businessservices, 1/3/2007.

24. *Multiple Employment and Training Programs, Funding and Performance Measures for Major Programs*, United States Government Accounting Office, GAO-03-589, April 2003.

25. Pink Magazine, November 2006, Page 93.

Glossary

Achievement Test—an instrument used to determine levels of proficiency in areas of learning such as reading, math, language.

Assistive (or Adaptive) Equipment—devices used to help people with disabilities to perform tasks that would not be possible without the accommodation of technology, for example a TDD (Telephone Device for the Deaf) machine.

Apprenticeship—planned, on-the-job training and instruction in all of the practical and theoretical aspects of a skilled occupation or craft.

Aptitude Test—a test instrument used to determine an individual's strengths and weaknesses in various cognitive areas including verbal, math, manual dexterity, spatial, and other areas, in order to predict future performance.

Assessment—a process of objectively discovering an individual's interests, aptitudes, and work values that can be used to develop career and job plans.

Barriers to Employment—conditions that may contribute to an individual having difficulty establishing strong attachments to the workforce. These include being a single parent or parenting youth, having a felony conviction, being a high school dropout, having a disability, speaking English as a second language, being a recipient of public assistance or food stamps.

Certification—documentation of having met approved standards, often by passing a test, to receive industry recognition in order to gain employment in the field.

Classroom Training—exchanging information and teaching/learning marketable skills utilizing a curriculum in a traditional class setting.

Customized Training—training to meet the individualized needs of a business or group of businesses that involves the contracted employment of an eligible new hire or group of new hires, allowing up to 50 percent reimbursement of the training expenses for a specified period of time.

Dislocated Worker—a worker whose employment with a company is terminated without the worker's initiation and who is eligible to receive unemployment insurance compensation.

Eligibility Determination—a process to ascertain if an individual meets the requirements to receive government-funded services. This may include proof of residence, income, nationality, age, immigration status, and/or Selective Service verification, depending on the dictates of the funding source or the local governing authority.

H-1B Visa—a nonimmigrant visa category of the Immigration and Nationality Act that allows American businesses to temporarily employ foreign workers who have the equivalent of a bachelor's degree in specialty occupations where there are skill shortages (nurses, engineers, etc.).

High School High Tech (HS/HT)—a Department of Labor program to provide opportunities for students with disabilities to get hands-on work experience in jobs in health-, science-, or math-related fields.

Incumbent Worker—a worker who is employed but meets specific requirements or works for a business that meets specific criteria established by a local workforce area to receive training assistance to upgrade skills.

Interest Inventory—an instrument used to explore an individual's preferences in performing career-or work-oriented tasks.

Internship—a paid or unpaid temporary work experience developed for the purpose of providing a student with hands-on skills training in a real work setting.

Job Readiness—the behavioral job-finding and job-keeping skills demonstrated by a job seeker.

JTPA—the Job Training Partnership Act, a piece of legislation enacted in 1979 to provide training and job placement assistance to eligible participants.

Labor Exchange Services—activities conducted by workforce development or employment service organizations that involve recruiting, screening, testing, and referring customers for hiring consideration.

On-the-Job Training (OJT)—contracted employment in the public, private, or nonprofit sector which allows up to 50 percent reimbursement of the wages of an eligible new hire for a specified period of time.

TANF (Temporary Assistance to Needy Families)-public assistance allotted to families with dependent children in the form of a cash allowance.

Tax Credit—a reduction in tax liability based on specific criteria as an incentive to engage in certain activities, for example the Earned Income Credit.

Unemployment Insurance Compensation—a temporary financial assistance, provided by state Departments of Labor, afforded individuals who are terminated from their jobs through no fault of their own.

WIA—the Workforce Investment Act of 1998 designed to create a comprehensive, customer-focused workforce investment system of integrated services provided by partnerships among multiple federal, state, and local organizations and agencies. The universal access of services to citizens is provided through the creation of One-Stop centers.

Work Experience—a temporary, try-out employment opportunity of limited duration for eligible program participants, usually without pay or at the minimum wage.

978-0-595-44133-4
0-595-44133-5

www.ingramcontent.com/pod-product-compliance
Lightning Source LLC
Chambersburg PA
CBHW020400290526
45785CB00005B/2377